GUINNESS WORLD RECORDS

ACTION PACK

W9-AWY-505

MIGHTY MICRO RECORDS

Compiled by Kris Hirschmann and Ryan Herndon

For Guinness World Records:
Laura Barrett, Craig Glenday, and Stuart Claxton

SCHOLASTIC INC.

New York   Toronto   London   Auckland   Sydney
Mexico City   New Delhi   Hong Kong   Buenos Aires

© 2006 Guinness World Records Limited, a HIT Entertainment Limited Company.

ISBN 0-439-88010-6

Designed by Michelle Martinez Design, Inc.
Photo Research by Els Rijper
Records from the Archives of Guinness World Records

12 11 10 9 8 7 6 5 4 3 2 1   6 7 8 9 10/0

Printed in China

First printing, October 2006

Visit Guinness World Records at www.guinnessworldrecords.com

Shrink down and think micro!

For more than 50 years, Guinness World Records has documented the most amazing record-breakers in every imaginable category. Today, their archives contain more than 40,000 entries.

Many record-holders make the biggest impact by being super small. This book takes a look at 15 record-holders of miniature proportions. Read about the **Smallest Lizard**, the **Smallest Dinosaur**, the **Smallest Motorcycle**, and much more. Then try the easy activities that explain the science behind the records. You can bring everything into focus by using the handy magnifying scope that comes with this book.

But wait — there's more! When you're done reading, test your memory with a trivia quiz about the mighty micro records featured in these pages. So **pay attention**. Not only will you ace the quiz, you'll also be able to dazzle your family and friends with facts about the records. And dazzling people, after all, is what Guinness World Records is all about!

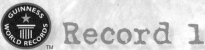

Record 1
Shortest Adult Actor
in a Leading Role

As a full-grown adult, Filipino actor Weng Wang (not pictured) stands only 2 feet 9 inches tall — the height of a typical 18-month-old boy. Wang made his film-acting debut when he was in his mid-twenties . . . playing a baby! The actor's big break came in 1979, when he starred in the James Bond spoof *For Your Height Only*. This role brought Wang lots of attention, including the record for **Shortest Adult Actor in a Leading Role**. As *Agent 00*, Wang (who has a black belt in karate) performed his own martial arts stunts. Wang went on to star in more hit movies, get married, and have five children — all of them taller than Dad!

Take Action

Tall Tales

Unusually short people sometimes have a hard time getting around in public places, which are designed for typical-height people.

Take a walk in a little person's shoes:

1. Put on some kneepads, if you have them.
2. Get down on your knees. Plan to stay there for the next 30 minutes while you go about your daily activities. How hard is it to do everyday things?

CHECK IT OUT!

American actor Verne Troyer (pictured in the middle on the opposite page and close-up above) is famous for his role as Mini-Me in the *Austin Powers* film series. Verne is one inch shorter than Weng Wang, but he has not yet received top billing on a project.

In 1998, Tom Wiberg of Sweden built the record-breaking **Tallest Motorcycle** (not pictured). What did he do for a follow-up? He built the **Smallest Motorcycle** (above and opposite page)! Wiberg introduced his mini-machine, "Smalltoe," in 2003. A model airplane engine powers the toy-size cycle. It has a front wheel diameter of 0.62 inches and a rear wheel diameter of 0.86 inches. The two wheels are only 3.14 inches apart, and the seat is 2.55 inches off the ground. This motorcycle cannot be ridden in the usual way (the photo on page 45 is posed). To qualify for the record, Wiberg "rode" his unique motorcycle about 36 feet with one foot on the seat. His wild ride never went faster than 1.2 miles per hour, the cycle's top speed.

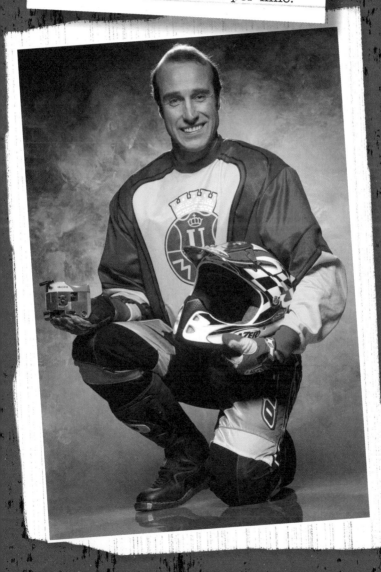

Take Action

Spin Cycle

Wheel size is one reason "Smalltoe" is much slower than a regular-size motorcycle. In one **revolution** (or complete spin of the wheel), smaller-size wheels cover less ground than larger ones. This fact limits the speed of small vehicles.

See how wheel size and speed work together:

1. Find a dime and a quarter. Use a permanent marker to make one dot on the edge of each coin.
2. Set the dime on a piece of paper, with the dot on the coin's bottom edge. Mark the paper below the dot.
3. Roll the dime until it has completed one full turn, then mark the paper below the dot again.
4. Repeat with the quarter.

Each coin made exactly one turn — but one coin traveled much farther than the other. Can you see why small wheels would need to spin faster to keep up?

magine driving a fairground bumper car on regular roads. Now imagine an actual car of about the same size! Before the Mini-Cooper cars came the Peel P50, built by Peel Engineering Co. on the Isle of Man, UK, between 1962 and 1965. The micro machine was 53 inches long, 39 inches wide, and 53 inches high. It weighed just 130 pounds. Designed to carry one person plus a shopping bag, the Smallest Street-Legal Car could reach speeds of 40 miles per hour. Unfortunately, the P50 never became a big seller because it was unstable, cramped, and noisy. Buyers also disliked that the vehicle could not go in reverse. To turn around, a driver had to get out of the car and rotate it by hand (above)!

Take Action

Super Strength

Even though the Peel P50 weighed 130 pounds, its front end was designed for one person to be able to lift it.

See for yourself how this worked by testing your bike at home:

1. With an adult watching, lift your entire bike all the way off the ground. A bit heavy, right?
2. Now lift the bike's front end only, leaving the rear tire on the ground. It's much easier! The rear tire supports some of the bike's weight, which means you have less work to do.

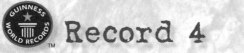

Record 4
Greatest Distance
Covered by a Miniature
Railway in 24 Hours

At Weston Park Railway in Shropshire, England, visitors can hop onto model trains one-eighth the size of regular trains. Steam-powered locomotives then pull the trains and their human cargo around a short track. Usually the locomotives are put away after a few hours of use. But between July 17 and 18, 1994, one coal-powered steam train named *Peggy* kept going for 24 hours straight. During this time, the 7.25-inch-gauge model train traveled 167.7 miles and snagged the record for **Greatest Distance Covered by a Miniature Railway in 24 Hours**. Ten different drivers took turns steering the locomotive in pursuit of the Guinness World Record. Today, *Peggy* can still chug along the tracks, although her passenger runs are limited to summer weekends (above).

Take Action

Tiny Traffic

You already know your magnifying scope makes tiny objects look larger. But did you know the same magnifying scope turned the opposite way makes objects nearby look smaller, too? Have fun using your magnifying scope to miniaturize the vehicles in your neighborhood!

To miniaturize your neighborhood:

1. Go outside. Look through the "wrong end" of your magnifying scope, or backward. The adjustable lens end should be against your eye.
2. Watch a car pass by. A real-size car will look like a toy!
3. Choose other objects to view through your scope. You have the power to shrink the entire world right there in your hands!

CHECK IT OUT!

A train track's **gauge** is the distance between the two metal rails. Standard train tracks have a gauge of 4 feet 8.5 inches.

Submarines come in many different shapes and sizes. The biggest military submarines can stay underwater for months and carry crews of nearly 200 people. At the other end of the scale are research subs, which are designed to take a few people underwater for a limited amount of time. At the farthest point among the research vessels is the *Water Beatle*, a one-person vessel that is the **Smallest Submarine** (above). This sturdy craft is only 9 feet 8 inches long, and 3 feet 9 inches wide. It is shorter than the average adult at 4 feet 8 inches high. Built by William Smith, the *Water Beatle* can dive to 100 feet and remain underwater for at least 4 hours using three air cylinders. The sub made its maiden voyage off the coast of Bognor Regis, England, in 1993.

Military subs are sometimes called "U-boats." This is an abbreviation of the German word **Unterseeboot**, which means "undersea boat."

Did you know?

The biggest Russian submarines have their own swimming pools.

Take Action

Up and Down

Submarines are able to rise and sink in the water because of a property called **buoyancy**. If a sub is positively buoyant, it rises. If negatively buoyant, it sinks. If neutrally buoyant, it stays level. The submarine controls its buoyancy by adding water (submerging) or releasing air (surfacing) from special tanks called **ballast tanks**.

See how buoyancy works with this simple experiment:

1. Find an **empty** 2-liter soda bottle and its lid. Get an adult to fill up the kitchen sink with water.
2. Screw the lid tightly onto the soda bottle. The bottle is full of air. Try to push the bottle into the water. The floating bottle is **positively buoyant**, unable to sink.
3. Remove the lid from the soda bottle. Fill the bottle with water. Replace the lid, then place the bottle in the sink again. Now the submerged bottle is **negatively buoyant**.
4. Adjust the amount of water until the bottle neither floats nor sinks to the bottom. This is **neutrally buoyant**. Your "sub" is ready for action!

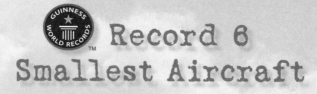

With a wingspan of 5 feet 5 inches and a nose-to-tail length of only 8 feet 10 inches, the miniscule biplane named *Bumble Bee II* didn't look like it could get off the ground. But the plane's designer and builder, Robert H. Starr of Tempe, Arizona, was convinced from the start that his creation would fly (above). The puny plane did exactly that on May 8, 1988, thus earning the Guinness World Record for the **Smallest Aircraft**. Powered by a large propeller, the *Bumble Bee II* climbed to a height of 400 feet and circled a field several times. The plane made several successful flights but eventually stalled and crashed during a takeoff. Although Starr was injured in the crash, he made a full recovery. The *Bumble Bee II*, unfortunately, was damaged beyond repair.

Take Action

Arms Out

Just how small was the *Bumble Bee II*? Consider the fact that most people can stretch their arms wider than the biplane's wingspan. An airplane you can hug — now *that's* an unusual idea!

See who makes the grade:

1. Ask a friend, and then an adult, to stretch his or her arms out to the sides.
2. Use a tape measure to find the distance from fingertip to fingertip.

Here's a hint: The arm span is usually less than a person's height. Anyone taller than 5 feet 6 inches has a good chance of passing your test!

Did you know?

The weight of the *Bumble Bee II* when empty was just 396 pounds.

Most predators are larger than their prey. This general rule holds true even for these two compact, winged hunters. The black-legged falconet (*Microhierax fringillarius*) from Southeast Asia (above) and the white-fronted or Bornean falconet (*M. latifrons*) from northwestern Borneo share the title of **Smallest Bird of Prey**. Both species measure between 5.5 and 6 inches, including a 2-inch tail, and weigh only about 1.25 ounces. They share similar hunting styles and meal preferences. Mice and other unsuspecting prey don't hear these birds power-diving from the sky at high speeds. Strong claws stun their prey, and sharper beaks finish off the meal.

Take Action

Raptor Watch

Ornithology is the scientific study of birds, but anybody can enjoy **bird-watching** — the activity of observing wild birds in nature.

Here's how you can go bird-watching:

1. Talk with a parent about going together on a bird-watching tour, joining a local bird-watching group, or taking a nature walk on a clear day.

2. Pack your magnifying scope, a field guide to the different types of birds, and a journal for "birding." Serious bird-watchers use binoculars, but you can still have fun with your handy magnifying scope.

3. Go to an area where birds are plentiful. Look through the eyepiece end of your magnifying scope for a close-up view of birds flying far away. What extra features do you see?

4. The biggest giveaway that you've spotted a bird of prey — or **raptor** — is a soaring bird. Raptors are excellent at coasting on air currents.

5. Take notes and use the field guide in identifying the birds you watched today.

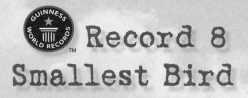

What delicate bird flits among the flowers, sipping nectar like a bee? If in Cuba, you would be admiring a bee hummingbird (*Mellisuga helenae*), the record-holder for **Smallest Bird** (above). Bee hummingbirds measure just 2.24 inches from beak tip to tail tip, and they weigh just over 0.05 ounces — that's lighter than a penny! These tiny fliers zip from flower to flower. When they find a plant they like, they hover in front of it, beating their wings so fast that the human eye perceives only a blur of motion. Then they use their long beaks and tongues to pull nectar and small insects from the plant. This sugary diet gives hummingbirds the rush of energy they need to keep on moving.

When hovering, the bee hummingbird's heart beats about 1,200 times per minute — equal to the shrew's regular heart rate, the **Fastest Heartbeat of Any Animal**.

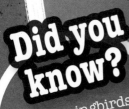

Did you know?

Hummingbirds are the only birds that can fly backward.

Take Action

Hummingbird Feeder

See hummingbirds in action by making your own backyard feeder! It might take a while for hummingbirds to find your place, so use your magnifying scope to watch the other types of birds flocking around your new feeder.

To make a feeder:

1. Paint the lid of a baby-food jar red. (Hummingbirds are drawn to red things.) Get an adult to poke several holes in the lid.
2. Fill the jar about three-quarters of the way with "nectar." To make nectar, dissolve ¼ cup of sugar in 1 cup of water.
3. Screw the jar's lid shut. Tie a string around the neck of the jar and hang it outside. Wait and watch. When hummingbirds show up, use your magnifying scope to get a look close-up!

Hang outside

Poke holes in lid

Fill jar with nectar

A fruit is the seed-bearing part of a flowering plant. Fruits come in an endless number of different shapes, colors — and yes, sizes! Are you surprised that the Smallest Fruit comes from the Smallest Flowering Plant? Two flowers from the floating duckweed plant *(Wolffia augusta)* of Australia could fit side by side inside a small letter o on this page. *W. augusta* floats on the surface of quiet ponds and streams (magnified, above). At certain times of the year, it produces fruit that is only 1/100th of an inch long and weighs about 1/400,000th of an ounce. That's about the same size as one grain of table salt! After ripening, these tiny fruits burst open to release the single seed inside.

Take Action

Magnify It

Microscopes are devices that help people study objects too small to look at with the normal human eye. Under a microscope, the size of tiny details and features is magnified by several times. You can use your magnifying scope just like a microscope and view some household items in a whole new way!

How to magnify the microscopic world:

1. Put a few grains of salt or dirt on a piece of paper.
2. You're going to use your magnifying scope "backward" again. Position the magnifying scope's eyepiece directly above the grains. (Place the object close to the lens for the best results.) You'll be amazed at how many tiny details are now large enough for you to see!
3. Find some other miniature objects to analyze — a strand of hair, the printed words in a book, spices, and breadcrumbs.

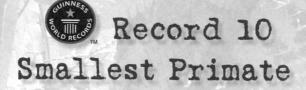

The primate family includes monkeys, apes, humans, and more. The runt of the family is the pygmy mouse lemur (*Microcebus myoxinus*), with a head-body length of about 2.4 inches, a tail length of 5.4 inches, and an average weight of 1.1 ounces. These miniscule measurements qualify for the **Smallest Primate** (above). Pygmy mouse lemurs live only on the island of Madagascar, discovered there in 1931. These mostly nocturnal primates hunt for grubs, fruit, flowers, and other tasty treats. During the day, they nap in leafy nests balanced on tree branches.

AREA OF DETAIL

MADAGASCAR

Indian
Ocean

AFRICA

South
Atlantic
Ocean

Fast Facts!

Three different species of the ever-growing lemur family were shown in the movie *Madagascar*, from left to right: ring-tailed, mouse, and aye-aye lemurs.

Take Action

Rule of Thumb

Like many primates (including humans), pygmy mouse lemurs have **opposable thumbs**. This means the thumbs can be turned opposite to the other fingers. Opposable thumbs help primates grasp objects while other, "thumb-less" animals find this task impossible.

Try to function without *your* opposable thumbs:

1. Ask a friend to tape each of your thumbs to its neighboring "pointer" finger, so your thumbs can't move independently.
2. Now, try to do these activities:
   - Use a pen to write your name
   - Turn the pages of a book
   - Use scissors to cut paper
   - Unscrew the lid of a jar
3. Were the activities easy, difficult, or impossible? Don't forget to remove the tape! You might need to ask your friend to help you with even this simple task.

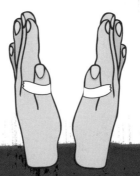

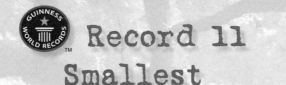

Look all you want, but you'll have a hard time spotting the pygmy shrew (*Suncus etruscus*). Also known as Savi's pygmy shrew, the **Smallest Burrowing Mammal** has an average body length of 1.4 to 2 inches with a tail length of 0.9 to 1 inch, and weighs between 0.5 and 0.9 ounces (above). It would take 15 to 20 pygmy shrews to equal the weight of one small mouse! Pygmy shrews need to eat constantly to keep their energy up, so they spend most of their time hunting for insects. Their food crawls by often, because these mammals are **burrowers** — a term for animals that live in holes dug in the earth. The tiny mammal takes shelter in the tunnels dug by large earthworms!

Take Action

How Heavy?

The biggest pygmy shrew found still weighs less than 1 ounce. What does a weight this light feel like?

The weight of each of these items is less than 1 ounce:

- 2 small paper clips

- 1 quarter

- 2 playing cards

- 1 vanilla wafer cookie

- 6 raisins

1. Pick up each item. Feel how light they weigh, separately and together.
2. What else can you find that weighs the same as, more than, or less than a pygmy shrew? Use a postal scale if you have one to continue the search on your own.

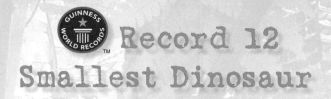

Not every dinosaur was gigantic. The **Smallest Dinosaur** was about the size of a chicken! *Compsognathus*, meaning "elegant jaw" in Greek, weighed only about 6.8 pounds and measured 2 feet from its lengthy snout to the tip of its long tail (replica above). In 1859, scientists dug up a nearly complete skeleton in Germany. (A second was later found in France.) The German skeleton proved that this dinosaur ate meat, not plants, because it contained a fossilized lizard — the last meal of this **carnivore** (fossil cast opposite page). *Compsognathus* lived during the Jurassic period, about 159 to 144 million years ago, and may have been a distant ancestor of today's birds. Some scientists even believe that *Compsognathus* was covered in downy feathers, but evidence proving this theory has not yet been found.

Compsognathus or "compies" (below) were featured in the movie *The Lost World: Jurassic Park.*

Did you know?

Compsognathus was the first birdlike dinosaur discovered. This discovery inspired scientists to explore the evolutionary link between dinosaurs and modern birds.

Take Action

Arms Out

Compsognathus stood upright on its two powerful hind legs. When running, its long tail helped it keep its balance. Today's birds, such as the peacock, use the same method. This principle is **counterbalance** — when an object's balance is maintained by placing equal weights on opposite sides. You don't have a tail, but you can use your "wings" to see how this works.

Flex your arms and test your counterbalance skills:

1. Cross your arms tightly over your chest, then stand on one foot. How long can you keep your balance without touching the other foot to the ground?
2. Now, try it the "compie" way! Stretch both arms out from your sides. Stand on one foot again. You will be amazed at your improved balance.

CHECK IT OUT!

Scientists who study dinosaurs are called **paleontologists**.

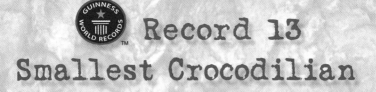

There are 23 species of crocodilians, a group that includes alligators, crocodiles, and gavials. The biggest crocodilians can grow to more than 20 feet in length. At the other end of the scale is the **Smallest Crocodilian** — the dwarf caiman of Central and South America (above). Females of *Paleosuchus palpebrosus* rarely grow longer than 4 feet while full-grown males measure at most 4 feet 11 inches in length. In the wild, adult caimans weigh between 13 and 15 pounds — about the same weight as an average house cat. These crocodilians are small in size, but their 82 needle-sharp teeth deliver a large amount of pain!

Take Action

Night and Day

An animal's eyes tell you plenty about its life. The **pupil** is a dark hole inside the eye's colored **iris**. The pupil's shape controls the amount of light entering the eye. Creatures active only in daytime (**diurnal**) or only at nighttime (**nocturnal**) often have round-shaped pupils. Creatures active during both night and day, however, often have slit-shaped pupils. Why? At night, slit pupils can open wider than round ones to let in the tiniest light rays from the moon. In daylight, slit pupils can close tighter than round ones to block the sun's bright rays. Night-roving creatures have highly sensitive eyes, so it is important to shield out too much sunlight.

See how the shape of an animal's pupil indicates its habits:

Go eye-to-eye with the caiman — with its photograph, that is (opposite page)! Judging by the shape of the pupil, when do you think caimans are most active? That's right! Caimans' slitted pupils help them move out and about in both sunshine and moonlight.

Open your eyes!

Study the pupils of your pets, animals at the zoo, and more photographs on the opposite page. Record if the pupils are round or slits. Research the animal's habits with the Internet, encyclopedias, and other sources and see what the eyes tell you!

What shape pupils does a caiman have? What shape pupils does an owl have?

Did you know?

The **Largest Eyes on a Mammal** belong to the Philippine tarsier (*Tarsius syrichta*). At a diameter of 0.6 inches, the tarsier's eyes would be equal to grapefruit-size eyes on a human.

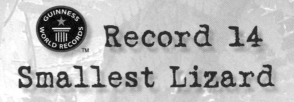

Two types of geckos share the Guinness World Record for **Smallest Lizard**. Both record-holders belong to the scientific genus *Sphaerodactylus*, which means "round fingers." *S. ariasae*, which was discovered in 2001, is found only on Beata Island near the West Indies (above). *S. parthenopion*, which was discovered in 1964, makes its home in the British Virgin Islands (not pictured). From snout to vent (not including the tail), these little lizards measure only 0.6 inches in length. *S. ariasae* and *S. parthenopion* are not just the micro-champs of the reptile world; they are tinier than all of the Earth's birds and mammals in this category.

Geckos don't have eyelids. Instead, transparent scales protect the eyeballs. Geckos use their long tongues to lick these scales whenever they want to clean their eyes.

Take Action

Get Wet

A smaller reptile loses moisture, or **dehydrates**, faster than a larger one because it has less body mass to contain water. Dwarf geckos often live in damp places to help their bodies stay wet longer. When studying these tiny reptiles, scientists make sure these creatures don't dry out and die.

See how dehydration works:

1. Find two sponges of different sizes and thicknesses.
2. Fill two separate pans with water and soak the sponges at the same time.
3. Remove the sponges from the pans, then place both wet sponges outside in a sunny spot.
4. Use a watch and time how fast it takes for the sponges to dry out. The sponge that stays wet longer has the best moisture retention.

Sponge

Water

Most Valuable
Single Stamp

Sold at auction on November 8, 1996, the "Treskilling" Yellow is by far the **Most Valuable Single Stamp** with a price tag of $2.3 million (above)! This Swedish stamp was produced in 1855. The series was supposed to be green with eight color tones ("eight-skilling"). But a mistake at the printers created a yellow stamp with three color tones ("three-skilling"). Although many of these "oops" stamps were printed, only one has survived to the present day. The printing error, combined with the stamp's "sole survivor" status, is the reason for the stamp's extraordinary price tag. In 2001, the "Treskilling" Yellow was back in the mail again for the first time in almost 150 years — this time *inside* the envelope. It was sent via registered post to the Nordia 2001 stamp show in Tucson, Arizona, where it was displayed for stamp collectors from around the world.

Take Action

Eye Spy

A stamp collector, or **philatelist**, often uses magnifying devices to look at their stamps. People look for printing faults or errors, folds, and damage to the stamp's **teeth** (the paper points that frame the stamp). These factors decrease a stamp's value. Collectors also use magnifiers simply to enjoy the fine details of a stamp's design.

See through the eyes of a philatelist:

1. Gather several different stamps. Place them on a flat surface.
2. You're going to use your magnifying scope "backward" again. Position the magnifying scope's eyepiece directly above a stamp. You're sure to discover many tiny details — and maybe even some mistakes — that you couldn't see before!

Fast Facts!

In stamp collecting, the term *EFO* describes everything that can go wrong with a stamp. *EFO* stands for "errors, freaks, and oddities."

Check Your FACTS!

How **good** is your **memory**?

You've read the records and done the activities. Now turn the page and answer 30 trivia questions about the information in this book. When you're done, check your answers on page 44.

① Shortest Adult Actor in a Leading Role

1. What country is the **Shortest Adult Actor in a Leading Role** from?
2. Weng Wang holds what color belt in the sport of karate?

② Smallest Motorcycle

1. What is the name of the **Smallest Motorcycle**?
2. Which travels farther in one revolution — a big tire or a small one?

③ Smallest Street-Legal Car

1. **True or false?** It was legal to drive a Peel P50 on regular roads.
2. Which gear did the Peel P50 lack?

④ Greatest Distance Covered by a Miniature Railway in 24 Hours

1. What is the name of the record-holding miniature locomotive?
2. This miniature train is about what fraction of the size of a standard train?

⑤ Smallest Submarine

1. *Water Beatle* is the name of a:
   a) Rescue boat   b) Submarine   c) Yacht
2. **True or false?** To sink, a sub lets air into special tanks.

⑥ Smallest Airplane

1. Was the *Bumble Bee II* a monoplane (one set of wings) or a biplane (two sets of wings)?
2. **True or false?** Most adults can stretch their arms wider than the wingspan of the *Bumble Bee II*.

⑦ Smallest Bird of Prey

1. **Raptor** is another word for what type of animal?
2. **True or false?** All predators are smaller than their prey.

Smallest Bird

1. Which item weighs less than a bee hummingbird?
   a) penny b) toaster c) sugar cube
2. What color attracts hummingbirds?

 Smallest Fruit and Flowering Plant

1. In what country is the **Smallest Flowering Plant** found?
2. How many seeds are found inside each *Wolffia augusta* fruit?

 Smallest Primate

1. Lemurs belong to which biological family?
2. What island is the home of the pygmy mouse lemur?

 Smallest Burrowing Mammal

1. What do pygmy shrews eat?
2. Pygmy shrews weigh less than:
   a) 0.1 ounce b) 1.0 ounce c) 10.0 ounces

12 **Smallest Dinosaur**

1. How many *Compsognathus* skeletons have scientists found?
2. Which animals today may be distantly related to *Compsognathus*?

13 **Smallest Crocodilian**

1. A dwarf caiman weighs about the same as:
   a) a guinea pig b) a cat c) a horse
2. On which continent are dwarf caimans found?

 Smallest Lizard

1. What type of lizard is the smallest?
2. What happens during dehydration?

15 **Most Valuable Single Stamp**

1. In stamp-collecting terms, what does *EFO* stand for?
2. What color was the **Most Valuable Single Stamp** *originally* supposed to be?

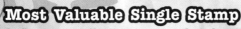

TRIVIA answers

Record 1
1. Weng Wang is from the Philippines.
2. Weng Wang holds a black belt in karate.

Record 2
1. "Smalltoe" is the mini-cycle's name.
2. A big tire travels farther than a small tire.

Record 3
1. **(True)** Driving the Peel P50 on regular roads was legal.
2. The Peel P50 lacked the reverse gear.

Record 4
1. *Peggy* is the name of the miniature record-setting locomotive.
2. *Peggy* is one-eighth the size of a standard train.

Record 5
1. **(b)** The **Smallest Submarine** is named the *Water Beatle*.
2. **(False)** To sink, a sub lets **water** into special tanks.

Record 6
1. The *Bumble Bee II* was a biplane.
2. **(True)** The biplane's wingspan was less than an adult human's arm length.

Record 7
1. **Raptor** is another word for a bird of prey.
2. **(False)** Most predators are larger than their prey.

Record 8
1. **(a)** A penny weighs less than a bee hummingbird's 0.05 ounces.
2. The color red attracts hummingbirds.

Record 9
1. Floating duckweed grows in Australia.
2. One fruit of *Wolffia augusta* yields just one seed.

Record 10
1. Lemurs belong to the primate family.
2. The pygmy mouse lemur lives on the island Madagascar.

Record 11
1. Pygmy shrews eat insects.
2. **(b)** Pygmy shrews weigh less than 1.0 ounce.

Record 12
1. Scientists have found two *Compsognathus* skeletons.
2. Scientists believe today's birds may be related to *Compsognathus*.

Record 13
1. **(b)** A cat and a dwarf caiman weigh about the same.
2. Dwarf caimans are found in South America.

Record 14
1. The gecko is the smallest type of lizard.
2. Dehydration is when a body loses moisture, dries out, and dies.

Record 15
1. *EFO* stands for "errors, freaks, and oddities."
2. The stamp's original color was to be green.

Congratulations! You magnified the possibilites!

Our book is nearly over — but your exploration of our record-breaking world doesn't end here. You can see more microscopic animals, machines, and objects among the online archives (www.guinnessworldrecords.com) and within the pages of *Guinness World Records* at your local library or bookstore. You're guaranteed to find thousands of extraordinary heights, lengths, weights, and widths stretching around the globe.

Think you've spotted a new contender in the microscopic world? Check out the official guidelines on page 47 about how your discovery can become a certified Guinness World Record. Maybe *your* name will appear in the next edition of the record books!

Photo Credits

How to be a Record-Breaker

Message from the Keeper of the Records:

Record-breakers are the ultimate in one way or another — the youngest, the oldest, the tallest, the smallest. So how do you get to be a record-breaker? Follow these important steps:

1.   Before you attempt your record, check with us to make sure your record is suitable and safe. Get your parents' permission. Next, contact one of our officials by using the record application form at *www.guinnessworldrecords.com*.

2.   Tell us about your idea. Give us as much information as you can, including what the record is, when you want to attempt it, where you'll be doing it, and other relevant information.

   a)   We will tell you if a record already exists, what safety guidelines you must follow during your attempt to break that record, and what evidence we need as proof that you completed your attempt.

   b)   If your idea is a brand-new record nobody has set yet, we need to make sure it meets our requirements. If it does, then we'll write official rules and safety guidelines specific to that record idea and make sure all attempts are made in the same way.

3.   Whether it is a new or existing record, we will send you the guidelines for your selected record. Once you receive these, you can make your attempt at any time. You do not need a Guinness World Record official at your attempt. But you do need to gather evidence. Find out more about the kind of evidence we need to see by visiting our website.

4.   Think you've already set or broken a record? Put all of your evidence as specified by the guidelines in an envelope and mail it to us at Guinness World Records.

5.   Our officials will investigate your claim fully — a process that can take a few weeks, depending on the number of claims we've received and how complex your record is.

6.   If you're successful, you will receive an official certificate that says you are now a Guinness World Record-holder!

Need more info? Check out the Kids' Zone on *www.guinnessworldrecords.com/ kidszone* for lots more hints, tips, and top record ideas that you can try at home or at school. Good luck!